HouseBeautiful
QUICK
Changes

HouseBeautiful

QUICK Changes

*Fresh Looks
for Every Room*

Edited by Barbara King

HEARST BOOKS
New York

HEARST BOOKS

New York

An Imprint of Sterling Publishing
387 Park Avenue South
New York, NY 10016

ISBN 978-1-61837-035-8

Distributed in Canada by Sterling Publishing

^{c}/o Canadian Manda Group, 165 Dufferin Street

Toronto, Ontario, Canada M6K 3H6

Distributed in the United Kingdom by GMC Distribution Services

Castle Place, 166 High Street, Lewes, East Sussex, England BN7 1XU

Distributed in Australia by Capricorn Link (Australia) Pty. Ltd.

P.O. Box 704, Windsor, NSW 2756, Australia

For information about custom editions, special sales, and premium and corporate purchases, please contact Sterling Special Sales at 800-805-5489 or specialsales@sterlingpublishing.com.

Manufactured in China

2 4 6 8 10 9 7 5 3 1

www.sterlingpublishing.com

CONTENTS

ACCESSORIZE it!

"Art on the walls is the one accessory I'd never part with. I'm not talking about expensive paintings, just works that you fall in love with. You cannot do without that in a house."

—Nancy Boszhardt

FLOOR-TO-CEILING

Remove all the pictures scattered around one room and rehang them on one wall, salon-style.

IN A GRID
To achieve the impact of a single large piece of art, hang a series of framed pieces.

DOMINATING A WALL

A tightly-assembled grid of prints creates a large, unified piece.

DESIGNER *tip!*

"Art doesn't have to be a huge investment. Cut out 20 pages from a favorite book. Buy 20 inexpensive frames and place them side by side in rows on a wall. Repetition is powerful."

—Orlando Diaz-Azcuy

TOP-TO-BOTTOM
Vertical grids elevate the sense of height in a room.

FILL A STAIRWAY WALL

"The way we hung these drawings and print in that seemingly random way—salon-style—has the feeling of those wonderful English country houses where they'd but some great oil painting and put it up where it fit," says Scott Sanders. "Oils would have been crazy-expensive and a bit overwhelming, so my best friend suggested we take a trip to Maine, where you can find inexpensive 19th-century charcoal drawings and prints. We bought 90 pieces, reframed and rematted them, and started hanging."

HANG JUST ONE BOLD THING

A red surfboard has a surprisingly powerful presence on a white stairway wall.

MAKE IT SHINE

Instead of art, hang a metallic hide on a wall behind the bed.

"Reflective finishes
bring a subtle,
pearlescent glow
to a room."

—Barry Dixon

◄ IN THE KITCHEN

If kitchens are the new living room, accessorize them like a living room! Hang art. Put a lamp or two on the counter. Put a rug on the floor—not just a mat. Here, photographs by Michael Belk hang over a Barry Dixon console illuminated by an Arts and Crafts lamp.

TABLETOP ➤ GALLERY

A console displays a grouping of art, photography and sculpture. The mini-easels give more stature to framed pieces.

THE PORTRAITS OF DUANE MICHALS 1958-1988

CREATE PRESENCE

Sculptural objects add another layer of visual interest. A large sphere with compelling graphic lines, a flea market find, dominates the coffee table in a living room. A torso-like piece of wood is mounted and displayed on a pedestal in front of the window.

DESIGNER *tip!*

"If I have a corner that's kind of dead, I'll make a rectangular pedestal out of plywood and lacquer it with high-gloss white paint. Anything you put on it, from a glass bowl to a concrete urn, suddenly becomes important. It's like a little museum installation."

—Frank Roop

ELEVATE ITS STATUS

A wooden pedestal holds a sculpture made of bristles from street sweepers, enlivening a corner in an entryway.

DIRECT THE EYE
A Dan Corbin sculpture on a small pedestal gains prominence in a living room and draws the eye toward the view.

BE BOLD

Patrick Wade put a ladder in his living room simply because he liked its scale and sculptural presence.

INSTANT EBAY COLLECTION

Magazine editor Zim Loy discovered Harkerware on eBay. "There's tons of it, and it's so cheap." Covering a dining room wall with plates has the same effect as the grid of framed prints on page 3: It reads as one big piece of art.

INSTANT TREASURE HUNT COLLECTION

Another magazine editor, Barbara King, found the prints hanging on her screen at an estate sale and a yard sale, the drawing propped on the window at a thrift shop, and the large portrait on the wall in a dusty, forgotten corner of a painter friend's studio.

MAKE YOUR OWN RULES

"There are no rules when it come to where collections can be displayed. Kitchens, baths, hallways, and stairwells can always use a little perking up," says design writer Frances Schultz.

FROM FASHION TO DÉCOR ACCESSORY

Take your jewelry out of the box. Show off your bracelets in a big glass bowl. Drape all your necklaces over a bust—it worked for Coco Chanel.

DESIGNER *tip!*

"Group collections —like things with like things. They look more important that way. And don't line objects up like they're on a march. Vary heights."

—Dan Marty

DISPLAY A COLLECTION ON A WALL

Wall brackets can bring order to a large collection or odd shapes, like these blue-and-white ginger jars.

STACK A COLLECTION

A library table holds stacks of books and a collection of blue-and-white porcelain.

◄ HIGH DRAMA

Plaster brackets holding a collection of celadon vases climb all the way up the wall to the high ceiling. Miles Redd wanted to replicate the look of a blue dining room wall displaying Chinese porcelain in Alex Vervoodt's 12-century castle.

A NEW TAKE ON A PHOTO ALBUM ➤

Black-and-white family photos in matching black frames lend graphic appeal to a hallway, and turn it into a place to linger and look.

THE ETERNAL APPEAL OF BOOKS

Even if you don't collect any particular type of book, do have books! A house is bereft without them. Artist Craig Schumacher's wall-to-wall shelves give his living room warmth and personality.

DESIGNER *tip!*

"Organize and style your bookshelves. Group books by subject or even color. Stand some upright, and then stack some horizontally to break the monotony. Mix in favorite pieces of pottery, collectibles, shells, or family photos."

—Angie Hranowsky

∧ GET INSPIRED

Stylist Aaron Hom thoughtfully arranges—
and rearranges—his bookcases with stacks
of design books and magazines, and objects
that inspire him: "To me, a big part of the
beauty of an object is what it's next to."

Turn one shelf over to a convenient bar. ➤

BOOKS BELONG IN EVERY ROOM!

A dining room with bookshelves always seems so much more inviting. (A banquette doesn't hurt, either.)

DESIGNER *tip!*

"Books are my favorite accessory because they're so personal— they reflect your interests. Stack art, design, gardening, travel books— whatever you collect—on a table."

—Joe Nye

SET UP A TABLE-FOR-TWO

Bring a dining room to your bookshelves! When they're alone, a Manhattan couple eats at a flip-top game table next to the shelves in their living room.

MAKE YOUR BOOKS MULTI-TASK

Stack coffee-table books next to a sofa for an instant side table.

"Do a photo mural in a foyer, at the end wall of a long, dreary hallway, or the ceiling of a tiny powder room, just for fun. Coloredgevisual.com or duggal.com have a great selection, or you can submit your own photo and they will scale it according to your wall."

—CHRISTOPHER COLEMAN

"Create the perfect picture wall. I organize my photos according to theme. I order frame and matting from thepicturewallcompany.com. They make it so easy that the photos practically arrange themselves on the wall."

—AMY LAU

"REINVENT FAMILY PHOTOGRAPHS. WE CONVERT ALL THOSE CHEESY CLOSE-UPS OF KIDS THROUGH THE DECADES TO BLACK-AND-WHITE. WE BLOW THEM UP, FRAME THEM ALL IN RED, AND DO A GIANT FAMILY WALL. WE LOVE TO DO FAMILY WALLS."

—KEN FULK

"If you have a dining table that stands dormant most of the time, turn it into a library table. Take beautiful books and create small stacks around the perimeter. Place a large-scale object like a piece of sculpture, or a fantastic topiary in the center. Then place a small object on top of each stack. Pick anything that interests you."

—THOMAS PHEASANT

"Display drawings in a color frame or in a white frame with a colored mat. Hang them in an otherwise unimaginative space. They're full of spirit—and meaningful."

—ERIC COHLER

"THERE IS NO REASON TO LIMIT FRAMED PICTURES ON YOUR DESK TO FAMILY PHOTOS. PRINT OUT A COPY OF YOUR FAVORITE PAINTING AND FRAME IT. IT WILL LIFT YOUR MOOD EVERY TIME YOU SEE IT."

—TIMOTHY CORRIGAN

"Buy clear acrylic plate stand for display. Anything you put on them becomes sculpture. Even terracotta tiles look like little paintings. Instant art."

—JEAN LARRETTE

"People have wonderful art books, but they rarely look at them. I bought a bookstand, set out one of my favorites, and now when I walk by I see a beautiful image. Turn the pages daily."

—PAUL VINCENT WISEMAN

NATURE'S BEST PATTERNS—NEVER OUT OF STYLE!

Tiger print on an ottoman gives a traditional room unexpected animal magnetism.

DESIGNER *tip!*

"I have a firm belief: every house should have at least one animal print."

—Kathleen Rivers

RUNNER
A zebra print adds pizazz to
any staircase.

DOUBLE ZING

And two big zebra print ottomans—topped with choice accessories in black lacquer trays—contribute to the drama of a living room by Martyn Lawrence Bullard.

SCREENS AS MINI-WALLS

Screens are one of the most clever accessories. They add texture and scale, another layer to a room. They can divide a small space into zones, act as a pretty disguise for stored items, add interest to a bare corner. Here, a screen divides the living and sleeping areas in a studio apartment.

DESIGNER *tip!*

"Make a folding screen. All you need is four pieces of plywood and some hinges. I did one for my office and upholstered it in linen, with cork on the other side so I can tack up pictures."

—Christopher Maya

FOR DEFINITION
◄ An upholstered screen studded with nailheads defines a living room bar area.

FOR ART
A screen adds architectural interest where there is none, and provides a "wall" for hanging art.

FOR COZINESS

A tall felt-covered screen marks a division between the living and dining rooms. The rooms are still open to each other, but the screen creates cozy, tucked-in corners on each side. In the living room, it provides a perfect spot for a mini-library. "I can't do anything without screens," says Miles Redd. "They do so much in terms of shifting a sense of space."

DESIGNER *tip!*

"We hung a two-panel Japanese screen over a recessed television to conceal it. The lightweight panels are easy to open and close, an important factor to keep in mind."

—Carey Maloney

ATLAS MAIOR

SCREENS AS ART

In the Martyn Lawrence Bullard living room, a silver-leafed screen makes a stunning piece of art and a focal point for the large room.

FILL YOUR HOUSE WITH FLOWERS

When it's not the season for lighting a fire, warm up that black hole with a big bunch of flowers. For even more beauty, add smaller arrangements to the mantel.

BATHE IN NATURE
Blooming branches brush an Amanda Weil photo on glass, which creates a window—and a flowering view—where there is none.

DRESS UP A WINDOW

Plant flowers in a window box. (Why not add more charm, and a French accent, by painting your windows Provence blue?)

DESIGNER *tip!*

"In summer, I plant two window boxes with especially fragrant herbs. When the breeze blows over them, the house is filled with scent."

—Clodagh

USE YOUR BEST THINGS NOW!

Start using your good silver and your fine china every day. As writer Joan Didion said, "Every day is all there is." Jewelry designer Federico de Vera sets his table with a trove of his exquisite Venetian glass: "If it breaks, it breaks. That's a gamble I'm willing to take because life's more pleasurable when you use beautiful things."

DESIGNER *tip!*

"It seems silly to have all that stuff just to be on display. Why not use the fanciest bowl for your cereal? I mean, what's it for?"

—Patrick Wade

THE BEAUTY AND VERSATILITY OF BASKETS

Photographer Victoria Pearson uses baskets to hold towels in her bathroom, and books in her bedroom.

And in magazine editor Zim Loy's bedroom, a basket holds pillows.

A Belgian laundry basket becomes a planter in a hallway outside a mudroom.

Tom Scheerer corralled barware and liquor bottles in a basket with matching napkin caddy: "I put it between the living and family rooms. Bars express welcome and conviviality, I like them out in the open."

"A HOUSE IS NOTHING WITHOUT THE ACCESSORIES. OTHERWISE ALL YOU HAVE IS A ROOM FULL OF FURNITURE."

—HATTIE WOLFE

"Something that has meaning to you—an object, a painting, a collection—is the personality that makes any room feel grounded and real, not some anonymous space."

—JEFFREY WEISMAN

"Nothing is worse than a big gorgeous room where they went for a bunch of 'stuff' just to fill in. There's no energy, no spirit, no life. It's filler. Accessories should represent the life of the person."

—CHARLOTTE MOSS

"GET SOME WICKER BASKETS AND FILL THEM WITH APPLES, PEARS, OR ENGLISH WALNUTS, DEPENDING ON THE SEASON, AND PUT THEM ALL AROUND THE HOUSE. THE MULTIPLICATION IS WHAT MAKES THE DRAMA."

—DAN CARITHERS

"Instant beauty: a bunch of magnolia leaves in a vase. And what's prettier and easier than a terra-cotta pot with a rosemary or French lavender plant?"

—LINDSAY REID

"Candlesticks in varying heights layer the light in a room—and can be beautiful objects in their own right."

—SUZANNE LOVELL

"BUY A PHOTOSPHORE— IT'S A VASE-LIKE CANDLE-HOLDER THAT YOU PUT VOTIVES IN, AND IT GIVES OFF A SOFT, ROMANTIC, DIFFUSED LIGHT THAT MAKES A ROOM LOOK SO WARM AND INVITING."

—SHERRILL CANET

"Get candles, and lots of them. They conjure romance instantly."

—RODERICK N. SHADE

PAINT*it!*

◀ BE DISTINCTIVE
Bold orange "keeps the
mudroom from looking
like your everyday
mudroom," says Mona
Ross Berman.

Sliding barn doors painted
the same vivid orange hide
the laundry area.

DESIGNER *tip!*

"For high drama, paint
the walls chocolate brown. For
something fresh, Hermes orange.
Go for a semi-gloss finish, which
gives life to the color."
—**Christopher Drake**

CLEAN AND FRESH

White walls update an old house.

MIMIC A RUG

Instead of using a rug in his tiny living room, designer David Kaihoi painted diagonal stripes on the floor, creating the effect of a graphic rug.

FAKE AN ENTRY

To designate an entrance, Kaihoi painted a small outlined square just inside the front door.

◄ ENVELOP A ROOM

Deep, glossy turquoise creates a chic cocoon in design writer Frances Schultz's guest room.

DON'T STOP THERE ➤

Schultz used the leftover turquoise paint to give the ceiling in her butler's pantry real atmosphere.

GO EVEN DARKER

Dark gray-blue on the walls and bookshelves creates a snug but sophisticated feeling in a family room.

GO ALL THE WAY!

"This little black lacquered box of a guest bath is everyone's favorite room," says Mark D. Sikes. "Very dramatic and sexy."

JUST ONE WALL

"I painted this staircase wall a vibrant Chinese red. Every time I see it, I feel totally exhilarated. And I won't put any art on the wall. That crisp high-gloss red is the artwork," says Amanda Kyser.

A NEW/OLD LOOK

Give your floor a new
look with paint... or
a historic one. Jeffery
Bilhuber painted his
library floor green, an
idea he borrowed
from Monticello.

CREATE CONTRAST

The floors in Kelly Van Patter's house were a mix of two kinds of wood. She unified them with a brown-black stain. "I wanted to have a really distinct difference between the walls and the flooring." She also stained the staircase steps.

ZIGZAGS ON THE FLOOR

Mona Ross Berman painted a zigzag pattern on the floor of a master bedroom. "It's a riff on a classic David Hicks pattern. My client says it reminds her of a Missoni dress. It creates impact without being overwhelming."

ZIGZAGS ON SHELVES
The herringbone pattern Christina Murphy painted behind bookshelves gives a living room its wow factor.

HIGHLIGHT OBJECTS

Jason Bell painted living room bookshelves—which are used more for display than books—a deep, earthy color.

"Paint the back of your shelves. But learn from my mistake: I just had to redo one because I chose a color that was too pale. It's dark back there, so you need a strong color, one with some punch."

—Ann Wolf

HIGHLIGHT COLLECTIONS

Ironstone and reliefware pops against the rich brown that was painted on the backs of these shelves. If it had been left white, or painted a pale color, the pitchers would have faded into the background.

CHEER UP YOUR BEDROOM
With pale yellow walls, a master bedroom conjures up its own sunny weather.

Brilliantly rich yellow in a custom mix intensifies the radiance of the morning sun in a bedroom.

DESIGNER *tip!*

"The best lighting trick in our house happens to be in our dining room, but you could do it wonderfully in a bedroom. The ceiling is high-gloss, in a shade of warm pink that my wife calls Never Need a Facelift. With candlelight, you get a color so romantic and sexy that I've joked about wanting to mirror the floorboards so I can see who's fooling around under the table."

—Alexander Julian

SET YOUR KITCHEN CABINETS AND ISLAND APART

Paint them in two different shades of the same color. Joe Lucas painted cabinets warm gray, and the island a cooler gray.

◄ PAINT FURNITURE

Magazine editor Zim Loy revamped her 1920s house with "lots of white paint," from all the walls to the dining room furniture. Besides the table and chairs (seen in the background), she painted a vintage sideboard white (and silver-leafed the top).

CLASSIC BLUE AND WHITE

Set off the island in a white kitchen with a friendly color like sea blue. And paint the backs of the open shelves in the same tone to set off your dishes and glassware.

THE FIFTH WALL
The high-gloss blue-gray ceiling reflects light, subtly giving this bedroom an understated radiance.

DESIGNER *tip!*

"Pick a predominant color from your room and paint the ceiling. It can be done in less than a day and a can of paint is so cheap!"

—Nathan Turner

PAINT IT GREEN
Apple green paint draws attention to beautifully displayed porcelains.

COLOR SATURATION

High-gloss dark green turns a small, modest kitchen into a gleaming jewel. Even the refrigerator was painted.

UPDATE VINTAGE
Every piece of furniture can't be brown. A Moroccan table gets a fresh spin with white paint. (And how about those walls? The power of pink!)

DESIGNER *tip!*

"Paint a piece of furniture the glossiest enamel paint you can find, and go for taxicab yellow or bright blue. Sometimes you need a shot of color that's unrelated to anything else in the house, for a surprise."

—Ann Wolf

Magazine editor Zim Loy painted a vintage sofa white and reupholstered it. "If the shape and size are right, I can paint it black or white and it will work for me."

◄ OPEN THE CABINET DOORS

An open armoire is more interesting than a closed one. Dan Marty lacquered his black, painted the interior, and created an interesting display with liquor bottles, baskets, art, books, pottery.

Mary McDonald turned an antique cabinet into a stunning bar. She ebonized the exterior and painted the inside red to glam it up.

PAINT YOUR BATHTUB

A bathroom is bathed in a silvery glow thanks to metallic paint on the walls, trim, ceiling, and yes, the tub.

BRING THE 18TH CENTURY INTO THE 21ST

In a young girl's bedroom, a Louis XVI-style dresser is given a modern, all-American treatment with red, white, and blue paint. And the door is given a signature Miles Redd treatment with leather and nailheads. He painted the chair yellow to match the lamps.

ROOM WITH A VIEW

Paint your window frames black. "Black gives the room a backbone, and it acts as a frame to the view," says Sally Markham. And in a room dominated by angles, add something round or curved for counterbalance.

"I believe in optimism and plenty of white paint."

—ELSIE DE WOLFE

"GIVE ONE ROOM A CEILING MAKEOVER. PAINT IT A FUN COLOR, THEN CHANGE A TRADITIONAL LIGHT FIXTURE TO SOMETHING BIG, MODERN, SPLASHY."

—MARY MCDONALD

"Don't dismiss your ceiling with white paint. The least you can do is tint it with a dollop or two of your wall color. Or paper it with pattern. Or make a sky of golden stars with rubber stamps and a metallic ink pad."

—LEE MELAHN

"IF YOU HAVE A ROOM PANELED IN NEW WOOD THAT IS TRYING TO LOOK OLD, TAKE A PAINTBRUSH AND ADD A THIN LINE OF BLACK IN THE FLUTES OF A COLUMN, OR ALONG THE RAISED PART OF A PANEL. THAT TOUCH OF BLACK WILL ADD AUTHENTICITY."

—TOM FLEMING

"Paint all the terra-cotta pots on your balcony or terrace with a polyurethane stain in high-gloss black or brown. They'll look like Chinese porcelain by the time you're finished."

—RANDALL BEALE

"PAINT CURTAIN RODS AND RINGS WITH A COLOR THAT COMPLEMENTS THE CURTAINS. RUB THE PAINT ON WITH A RAG: IT CREATES A SOFTER EFFECT."

—JIM HOWARD

"In a New York bachelor pad, we painted all the doors a beautiful charcoal gray—something I do frequently when the architecture isn't great."

—RUTHIE SOMMERS

"PAINT YOUR BASEBOARDS A CONTRASTING COLOR SUCH AS SPANISH BROWN OR DARK GRAY. IT'S LIKE APPLYING EYELINER—IT WILL MAKE THE WALL POP."

—THOMAS JAYNE

WALLPAPER *it!*

TROMPE L'OEIL
In Stephen Shubel's bedroom, Genuine Fake Books wallpaper creates the illusion of more space.

IT DOESN'T HAVE TO BE PERFECT

David Kaihoi papered his bedroom with pieces of antique wallpaper he bought at an auction. There's fading, there's patching, but there's no denying it still looks beautiful.

MAKE IT SAY "WELCOME!"

Designer Tobi Fairley used Nina Campbell's Veneziano: "It's a fabulous damask print, traditional but so overscale that it's modern and fresh." She added a shot of vivid blue with Venetian glass lamps from Swank Lighting.

DESIGNER *tip!*

"Wallpaper your front entry with a bold paper. It creates a strong first impression and makes it seem like you have done a total makeover."

—Peter Dunham

A MASCULINE TOUCH

Paper one wall in pinstripe. "It adds depth and texture," says Ken Fulk. Here, it also "provides relief from the heavily ornamented bed." (Take note: Antique Asian hatboxes stacked with books serve as night tables.)

◀ ENERGIZE CLOSET DOORS

The fastest way to make over sliding closet doors is to wallpaper them. Melissa Warner chose a bold graphic for a big splash of color and pattern for a bedroom-turned-home office.

DESIGNER *tip!*

"Wallpaper a closet. A linen closet only needs a couple of rolls and you will feel sheer joy every time you open it."
—Ruthie Sommers

ENERGIZE BOOKSHELVES ▶

Ann Wolf lined the back of shelves with marbleized wallpaper. "And sometimes I do wallpaper on a ceiling. It's easy. But you have to be careful not to pick a pattern that's directional. No patterns where you have to stand one way to see it, like a toile."

INVENT YOUR OWN WALLPAPER

Old letters paper the back of an antique French cabinet. So take those love letters out of the shoe box, and let the world know how romantic you are!

ENVELOP THE WALLS

Designer Kevin Isbell wrapped the master bedroom in a deep-colored grass cloth to make it cozy. "Grass cloth has a warmth that paint does not, and darker colors are more cocoon-like." As a counterpoint to the floral curtains, he applied grosgrain ribbon in a graphic pattern to the sofa's white upholstery.

GO FOR TEXTURE

Ken Fulk jazzed up a chimney breast with black crocodile wallpaper. "It looks great, that texture. And it's fun."

DESIGNER *tip!*

"Paper the back of a cabinet or bookshelf in faux snakeskin, crocodile, or ostrich. Paint can't come close to the impact. It will inspire you to rearrange your shelves."

—Jean Larrette

FROM PLAIN JANE TO PRETTY

This powder room was ordinary and forgettable before Kristin Panich turned it into a beauty queen with wall-to-wall orchids.

DRAMA BEGINS IN THE FOYER

Black vinyl wallcovering mimics lacquer and "fools everyone," says Rob Southern. For theatrical contrast, the English hall chairs are painted white.

FLORAL BACKDROP
Vintage wallpaper gives an old-world elegance to a bar set up on a childhood desk.

MAKE YOUR KITCHEN CEILING SING

This one is painted (not a quick change!) but you can achieve the same effect with wallcovering.

GO FOR IT! ➤

"Powder rooms are places where you can gild the lily," says Mona Ross Berman. "We used a loud geometric in a bright ocean blue to give it a slightly over-the-top feeling."

◄ **BLACK PATENT**

An ordinary hallway becomes super-chic when it's covered in high-gloss black wallpaper. An étagère holding books and white ceramics provides an arresting focal point for the end of the hall.

MIRROR*it!*

MIRRORED PANELS

Images reflect back and forth in a dining room. Orlando Diaz-Azcuy mirrored panels on opposite walls, creating an exciting, entrancing atmosphere. "You see the guests and the lights from the sconces and candles in infinitesimo images. It makes the simplest dinner feel glamorous."

DESIGNER *tip!*

"Mirrors are the least expensive way to give a space a luxurious feel."

—Orlando Diaz-Azcuy

◄ MIRRORED WALLS
Mirrors on opposite walls in a Martyn Lawrence Bullard bathroom expand the room and reflect light.

DOUBLE REFLECTION ➤
Vicente Wolf put an Italian desk in front of a massive framed mirror that he leaned against the wall: "It's like an entrance into another room."

SPACE ENHANCER

Mirrored cabinets in a small bedroom expand the sense of space. And that curtain! Couldn't be simpler.

DESIGNER *tip!*

"A mirror makes a fabulous backdrop for art. I love to prop a painting in front, or hang it right on top."

—Robert Brown

TWO ARE BETTER THAN ONE

Two large mirrors that meet in a corner of a family room "open up the space and bring the outdoors in," says Vicente Wolf. "They also add depth and substance."

OPEN THE ROOM
Don't be afraid to put a big mirror in a small room. It enhances the sense of scale.

WAKE IT UP

Antiqued mirrored glass on cabinet doors animate a small Jonathan Berger kitchen.

DESIGNER *tip!*

"Inset mirrors into the panels on a door. I did it in my dining room and my bedroom, and it perks up the whole house."

—Pat Healing

GIVE IT A BEGUILING LOOK

Panels of antiqued mirrors on Frank DelleDonne's closet doors add
"a little bit of smokiness and mystery" to his bedroom.

KITCHEN MAGIC

An antique mirror turns a wall over a stove into a window, and makes the kitchen feel like a beautiful dining room.

OLD-WORLD ELEGANCE

An antique mirror is propped behind the silvered tub in a guest bathroom.

HOLLYWOOD GLAM
Mirrored chests and a starburst mirror add glamorous luster to a bedroom.

AS DAZZLING AS A DIAMOND

A mirrored vanity—and pearlescent tiles—turns a powder room into a sparkling jewelbox.

DESIGNER *tip!*

"Find a great antique mirror for your powder room. The slight mottling of glass seems to make those tiny lines and wrinkles miraculously disappear. And when people know they look great, they have more fun."

—Ashley Whitaker

FRAME ART IN MIRRORS

Mirrored bedside tables and mirrored frames give a crisp blue and white bedroom just the right touch of luminosity.

WHEN IN DOUBT

You can never go wrong with a starburst mirror. Use it anywhere—over a mantel, a bed, an entry table. "I'll always have a starburst in my life," say Meg Braff.

DESIGNER *tip!*

"I bought a cheap starburst mirror, gilded parts of it to make it look richer, and screwed it to the ceiling. It's dazzling."
—Benjamin Dhong

◄ HANG A MIRROR ON A BOOKSHELF

Designer Mary McDonald hung a mirror on a display cabinet exquisitely arranged with books and a collection of white sculptural objects, with a little gilt thrown in for elegant sparkle.

RADIANT TABLES ➤

Mirrored tables double the beauty of flowers and bounce light up to the ceiling.

HANG A MIRROR OUTSIDE

An oversize mirror—and filmy white curtains—take a veranda from comfortable to dreamy. "The veranda is more of an enclosure like this: it transports you," says Bill Brockschmidt. "The curtains change the mood, depending on whether they're tied back or not, or closed completely. They have a breezy feeling, and they make the outdoor space seem cooler. In warm weather, the veranda is the family room."

"I've always been fascinated with mirrors: I find them so glamorous, and they expand the space. A mirrored screen can transform a room from drab to fabulous in an instant. Attached to one side of a nook, it creates a door: Voila! Hidden storage for linens, luggage, even a TV. A mirrored backsplash can give a small kitchen a larger, lighter feeling."

—NANCY CORZINE

"Place a large mirror opposite a window to open up a room and double the amount of natural light."

—JEFF ANDREWS

"I LOVE PUTTING MIRRORS IN BUILT-IN CABINETRY. I HAVE MIRRORED GLASS IN THE PILASTERS SEPARATING THE BAYS OF BOOKS IN MY LIBRARY/DINING ROOM, AND THE EFFECT AT NIGHT DURING A DINNER PARTY IS INCREDIBLE. THE MIRRORS REFLECT THE SHIMMERING LIGHT OF THE CHANDELIER, BOUNCING IT ALL AROUND THE ROOM."

—JONATHAN BERGER

"IN MY APARTMENT, I USED A VERY LARGE MIRROR TO EXAGGERATE THE SIZE OF MY DINING ROOM. THE LARGER THE MIRROR, THE LARGER THE IMPACT. JUST BE SURE IT'S OPPOSITE SOMETHING YOU DON'T MIND SEEING!"

—MARIETTE HIMES GOMEZ

"In an entry, I mounted antiqued mirror on all four walls. It glowed like a light-box. Mirror Fair [mirrorfair.com] has the best-quality 'old' glass."

—CAREY MALONEY

"MIRROR THE INSIDE OF YOUR WINDOW-FRAME: IT WILL FEEL LIKE A BAY WINDOW."

—ERIC COHLER

"In a room with ceiling-to-floor curtains, I mirrored the wall above the top of the window. It filled that sad, blank space and extended the window in a romantic, luminous way. I used acrylic mirror—it's not as heavy as real mirror—and hung it with double-sided tape."

—RICHARD MISHAAN

"I use mirrors everywhere because they bring light into a space. I like to have them cut in simple panels, like a trumeau, without the decorative elements. It's a way of giving an old craft a modern twist."

—BARBARA BARRY

COZY IT *up!*

LIVING ROOM

What room doesn't benefit from a chaise? David Netto amped up the coziness quotient in a beach house living room with a fireside chaise.

FAMILY ROOM

A chaise in a family room is the perfect perch for settling in and watching TV, which is placed in a no-fuss way on the bookcase ledge. "TVs are so good-looking now, we don't have to hide them," says Markham Roberts. This means we no longer have to measure out niches or construct hideously huge mechanized ottomans at the foot of the bed that lift up the television like Dracula's coffin."

MASTER BEDROOM
A chaise at the end of a bed adds to this room's nested feeling.

GUEST ROOM
Your guests will be pampered by a luxurious chaise lounge.

THINK BEYOND YOUR WINDOWS

Draw the curtains, and a children's reading room becomes a private hideaway. "It's a niche carved out of a hallway," says Ann Wolf, "a very private, magical world, like being in a tent." It also doubles as a guest room for sleepovers. "We used grommets on the curtains so that it could be totally closed off. If you do rings, you're going to get space at the top, but with grommets, the fabric goes all the way up to the ceiling. The other side of the curtain is a different fabric, the same as on the square pillows."

◄ A basement nook was turned into a guest room, with curtains providing privacy.

BED PLUS SOFA ➤

Instead of the standard single or double bed in a guest room, put in a day bed, with pillows lined up against the wall. Voila! It's a living room by day, bedroom by night. Note the coffee table: Lucite disappears, making any room feel airier.

FURNISH YOUR BATHROOM! ➤

Why shouldn't your bathroom be as inviting as the rest of your house? Use a rug instead of a bath mat. It was made to withstand a lot more wear than the occasional wet foot. Lean art on a window sill. And if you have the space, put in a comfortable chair.

BRING THE INDOORS OUT

Roll-arm sofas and chairs in Perennials fabrics makes an outdoor living room "look like indoor furniture has been dragged outside," says Martyn Lawrence Bullard.

OUTDOOR ENTERTAINMENT

Put a TV in an outdoor room. It will become everyone's favorite gathering spot.

CATER TO THE ➤
WHOLE FAMILY
A kitchen chalkboard
is great for making
grocery lists, doing
math problems, or
even drawing
a mural.

◄ ALFRESCO
DINING
Put a table outside—
any old table—drape it
with a white cloth, and
enjoy the fresh air.

IN THE KITCHEN ➤

Barry Dixon cantilevered a custom lazy susan table with a hammered metal top over the kitchen island, creating a casually elegant spot for family meals.

◄ ON THE WALL

Hang your pots and pans on a wall, as designer Jeffrey Bilhuber did in his kitchen (but skip the Julia Child pegboard). It's useful and homey.

TRANSFORM AN AWKWARD SPACE

A barren corner underneath the foyer stairwell became a surprisingly cozy nook when Melissa Rufty added a banquette and coffee table: "That's one of my favorite spots in the house. It sets a welcoming, relaxed tone. When we have a party, it starts out collecting coats and purses, but it ends up collecting the late-nighters."

SWATH THE ROOM
Flax curtains extend all the way over to the bookshelves next to the bed, making it possible to cocoon the bedroom in fabric.

◄ FOOT OF THE BED

Instead of a bench, create an inviting seating area.

PUNCH IT *up!*

PILE IT ON!

"I can't live without color," says Kathryn Ireland, who layered a bed with brilliantly colored pillows and a patchwork quilt. "I use a lot of ethnic textiles, because they work anywhere."

COLOR PUNCH

Bright colors and dynamic patterns bring a white living room to life. The yellow leather poufs also "make great extra seating," says Mona Ross Berman, "especially for kids."

NATURAL BEAUTY

A turquoise lamp is like a discrete piece of jewelry in an all-neutral, all-wood room.

DESIGNER *tip!*

"Every room has to have one big pop of color."
—Kelly Van Patter

INSTANT COLOR

A zippy color makes your fireplace a focal point. Ashley Whitaker used a sea blue.

DESIGNER *tip!*

"Add a splash of red to your room. It could be a lampshade, a cushion, a rug with some red in the pattern. Red is so uplifting."

—Kathryn M. Ireland

SPLASH RED EVERYWHERE

Roman Alonso uplifted his living room with the oversize red lampshade, the red rug, red accents in the pillows and the blur of red in the Lisa Eisner photo. Alonso ran out of wall space, so he propped black and white photos on the floor: "It's like wainscoting." His sofa is simply a twin mattress and box spring covered in painter's linen.

GLAMOROUS RED

Designer Mary McDonald lacquered her large walk-in closet red and created a glamorous vanity at one end.

DESIGNER *tip!*

"Buy an inexpensive paper lampshade and paint it red. It makes the light incredibly romantic and flattering."
—Joe Nye

ALL-AMERICAN RED
And look what red did for David Kaihoi's modest little bedroom closet.

DESIGNER *tip!*

"In one house, I put red felt and nailheads on all the doors. Felt is good because it's sturdy—you touch doors a lot, bang things into them. I love its deepness, and the colors it comes in."

—Peter Dunham

BE DARING FROM THE GET-GO
A bench upholstered in vivid purple makes a strong color statement in the entry.

Miles Redd revved up a hallway with doors covered in green leather and nailhead trim.

DESIGNER *tip!*

"Upholster an ordinary hollow-core door in leather, or one of the new vinyls that look like leather. If you have the patience, add nailheads in a geometric pattern."

—Marshall Watson

GRAPHIC WOW FACTOR

No one who sleeps in this guest room will ever forget it. "Stripes have an amazing power to instantly transform a room," says Ken Fulk, who had them painted horizontally, in wide black and white.

Carleton Varney dramatized an entry—and summoned the spirit of Dorothy Draper—by striping the walls in black-and-white vertical stripes. (And note the zebra-print runner.)

DESIGNER *tip!*

"If a room doesn't have that much going for it, I tart it up with something bold, like striped walls."

—Peter Dunham

◄ MAKE THEM COLORFUL

The stripes in the guest bath mimic a cabana, and they're also a distraction from the room's awkward shape.

DESIGNER *tip!*

"Paint stripes on your ceiling. They create movement and energy. It's a delightful surprise."

—Kelly Wearstler

MAKE A DISTINCTION ➤

Painted stripes delineate the living area from the kitchen in an open-plan cabin.

STRIPE A LAMPSHADE

The black-and-white shade in Stephen Shubel's kitchen gives an antique gilded lamp a modern twist.

PATCHED STRIPES

In a dining room, a vintage striped patchwork rug under the table is in keeping with the natural aesthetic.

GENTLEMANLY COTTAGE

Painted stripes add pizzazz to a tiny room that combines living, dining and kitchen areas.

STRIPE A LAMP BASE

And paint stars on the shade.
Eric Cohler's shades echo the
lively suzani on his bed.

DESIGNER *tip!*

"People don't often
think of it, but you can paint
a flat linen or silk shade. I like
stripes, but you could use
stencils, too. I think it makes a
room look very designer-y
and kind of European."

—Ann Wolf

MAKE YOUR OWN STRIPED RUG

Designer Heather Moore
created a randomly
striped bedroom rug
by piecing together two
Karastan colors.

DESIGNER *tip!*

"Get a carpet
remnant and put it
down in an unusual
place, like a patio or
balcony. Or take up
some of your rugs.
Bare wood and stone
floors can be just
as beautiful."
—Eric Cohler

A SINGLE STRIPE

A throw in a darker neutral lends depth to a linen-covered settee, which Benjamin Dhong paired with a block table. "Not only is the juxtaposition pleasing, but I love the way small silver trays look on the block."

TEXTILE UPLIFT

A vintage Suzani adds
a vibrant punch to a
neutral sofa. Stacked
coffee table books find
a second home on the
large ottoman.

PATTERNED AND PLEATED

Dan Marty turned ginger jars into
lamps for his living room, and made
the shades with vintage fabrics.

"Colored, patterned
lampshades are among my reliably quick
ways to deliver punch to any space."

—Kathryn M. Ireland

ADD SPARKLE

One dazzling lamp can transform a room. Heather Moore had this lavender silk shade lined in deep amethyst and did a larger-than-usual box pleat for a more contemporary look.

PATTERN A KITCHEN SHADE

A pendant light sports the same fresh, overscale fabric as the chairs. For more color in the white kitchen, designer Jonathan Adler amply stocked the open shelves with blue dishes.

GRAPHIC PUNCH

Upholster a headboard in a zippy geometric. At the foot of this guest-room bed, a hotel-worthy touch: a Waldo's Designs desk and armchair. "Everyone has a laptop," Joe Lucas says. "Even guests need a place to work."

OVERSCALE FLORA

David Netto covered the wall behind a guest room bed in a dynamic fabric. "The smaller the room, the more drama you need," he says. "The Svenskt Tenn Hawaii fabric by Josef Frank is so bold, it creates a little world within the bed alcove. Guests feel like they're sleeping in an enchanted garden."

INDULGE A FANTASY

Change your standard-issue headboard to one that's fanciful and exotic: it'll bring romance to your bedroom!

"I WAS ASKED TO ASSIST A FRIEND WHO HAD AN INCREDIBLY BLAND LIVING ROOM. IT LACKED SOUL. I HAD THE WALL BEHIND THE SOFA PAINTED FIERY RED, AND BOUGHT THREE PILLOWS FOR THE SOFA—RED, ORANGE, AND FUSCHSIA. THE ROOM CAME TO LIFE."

—JAMIE DRAKE

"If you have something with great shape but not quite enough dash—a lamp, a table, even a chair—take it to your framer and have them gild it."

—JEFFREY WEISMAN

"Change the color of your lampshades to black. Much more dramatic, and it creates lovely pools of light—along with a little punctuation—in a room. Line the shades in gold paper to add a little sparkle."

—JENNIFER GARRIGUES

"THE DOORS OF MY BEDROOM AND MY KIDS' ROOM FEEL VERY CHEAP AND FLIMSY. I'M ABOUT TO COVER THEM IN A TAUPE BURLAP. THEN I"LL PAINT THE MOLDING DETAILS IN A MUD-COLORED STRIE. I EXPECT THEM TO GAIN A BIT OF DISTINC-TION AND THE HUMBLE DIGNITY THAT BURLAP SEEMS TO GIVE WHATEVER IT COVERS."

—CELERIE KEMBLE

"In a showhouse, we were given a plain door with two-by-fours for trim. It needed oomph, so we drew a fluted pilaster around it and a pediment above. We painted freehand over the drawing in white. It reminded me of line drawings in all those charming **Madeline** books."

—ANN DUPUY

"Paint your living room doors Chinese red with a high-gloss finish, and slipcover the sofa in red and white mattress ticking. The result will be young and vibrant."

—DAVID KLEINBERG

"If you live in a ho-hum space without any architectural details like crown moldings, do what I did. Apply a 1" tape to the perimeter of your ceiling—you can buy inexpensive masking tape from an art supply store in an array of colors. Inset the tape 1" to 1½" away from the wall. Follow any natural turns that result from soffits or columns. The result is a crisp, clean outline that adds height and defines the space."

—JONATHAN ROSEN

REFRESH*it!*

REINVENTING AN AMERICAN CLASSIC

Lindsey Reid slipcovered her black Windsor dining chairs with a zesty ikat polka dot fabric. "It makes them look younger, and it brings them to life."

EASY BREEZY

A fast-fix casual look for dining chairs: slipcovers made of vintage grain sacks. And it doesn't get any simpler than those curtains. "I think of them as dishrags on cup hooks," says Jesse Carrier. "They're Sunbrella panels. You can just unhook one of the corners and let it drop."

DESIGNER *tip!*

"Take a dull set of dining chairs and spray-paint them black. Then splurge on a glorious fabric to cover the seats. Or what about pink patent leather?"

—Ken Fulk

◄ REINVENTING A FRENCH CLASSIC

Louis XVI- style chairs upholstered in a Robert Kime Asian-inspired pattern give a breakfast room an elegant global look.

CHANGE THE BACKS OF CHAIRS ➤

Reupholster them in a different, but harmonious, fabric.

◄ **LOVE YOUR CLOSETS**
Paint them, paper them, hang pictures in them to inspire you. And definitely light them.

SKIRT A TABLE

A skirt can dress up a table, hide all your junk, add a feminine touch. The skirted table in this room has a flap on the bed side that flips up to reveal a hidden bookshelf.

SKIRT A BATHROOM SINK
Windsor Smith wrapped her bathroom
sink in striped silk, both dressing it up
and adding feminine flounce.

SKIRT THE SINK AND THE WALL

Instead of ripping out unsightly tilework, T. Keller Donovan rehabilitated it with a pleated cotton stripe hung from ceiling mounted hospital track—and draped it around the sink.

DON'T TOSS IT, REIMAGINE IT

Ann Wolf's client thought she would have to buy a new dining table for her newly fresh, young dining room, painted in vibrant green. "Because it wasn't super-fine, we just stripped and bleached it for an updated look," says Wolf. The client also wanted to get rid of the glass lamps. "She'd had them for a long time. But I convinced her that we should just change the shades. It gave them a whole new look."

MOVE THINGS AROUND

Turn two chairs in opposite directions, flanking an ottoman—you'll have a modern version of the French tete-a-tete. To make a living room feel larger, Barry Dixon arranged the club chairs and ottoman in a diagonal—the longest line in a square room.

REARRANGE THE WHOLE ROOM

If your living room is large, divide it
into distinct seating areas. Add an extra
coffee table or two.

"Bringing in one new
piece can take a room in a
whole new direction."

—James Swan

MIX UP THE SEATING

"I'd never, ever put eight matching chairs around a dining table," says Vicente Wolf. "You wouldn't have eight chairs all exactly the same in your living room, would you?" This dining room is small, so he used a banquette and ottoman to seat as many people as possible.

MIX AND MATCH
Even in a formal
dining room, mixing
the chairs adds interest
and charm.

RETHINK FIREPLACE
SEATING ➤
Move your sofa and coffee table
away from the fireplace. Try
two armchairs with an ottoman
between them. Much cozier.

ANGLE FURNITURE

Setting furniture and a rug on an angle changes the whole dynamic of a room.

FLOAT FURNITURE

Stylist Ellen O'Neill floated her bed in the middle of the room because "out that window is a great view of an unmown field, and I wanted to lie here and look at it."

DESIGNER *tip!*

"Floating furniture can create the illusion of a larger space. Furniture against a wall can feel cold sometimes, like a high school dance where everybody is standing around the perimeter of the gym."

—Vicente Wolf

ADD A MODERN TWIST

Abstract art looks right at home in this mix of traditional and antique furniture.

WHY NOT BUY A SAARINEN TABLE?

It works in any room, with any style, anywhere. And it looks right no matter what kind of chairs you pair it with. Tom Scheerer mixed a Saarinen coffee table with a Victorian-style sofa and antique Bar Harbor wicker chairs in the living room of a New England summer house.

⋀ IN A LIVING ROOM

Vernon Panton C1 chairs surround a wood-topped Saarinen table in broker Royce Pinkwater's living room. And check out the cozy chaise by the window.

IN A DINING ROOM

Saarinen's oval table and executive armchairs make Bonnie and John Edelman's dining room in Ridgefield, Connecticut immensely hospitable. "Eero Saarinen gets my total respect for designing a table where people can sit without the annoyance of table legs," Bonnie says.

A Saarinen marble-topped table and Tulip chairs are right at home in the dining room Aaron Hom's Craftsroom Bungalow and in a family room designed by Benjamin Dhong, both in San Francisco.

⋀ The Saarinen table in Lindsey Bond's Birningham, Alabama dining cottage is paired with antique klismos chairs. Draw inspiration from her many quick fixes: The interior curtain separating her dining area from the living area. The accent wall. The architectural mirror. The sisal rug. The white hide layered on the sisal. A banquette that's simply a long bench with a lumbar pillow.

IN A BREAKFAST ROOM

Smith Hanes made a breakfast room in Chatahoochee Hill, Georgia richly cozy
and elegant with a vintage Saarinen table, Vine Oly studio chairs, and walls
painted deep brown.

IN A SUNROOM
A vintage Saarinen table is paired with antique Chinese chairs in photographer Amy Neunsinger's indoor-outdoor L.A. sunroom. (Take note: She enlivened a big expanse of white wall with a collage of photos in various frames—some hanging, some leaning on a shelf and the floor.)

SOFTEN THE AUSTERE
Bring in a round table or
natural wood furniture.

DESIGNER
tip!

"Floating furniture can
create the illusion of a larger
space. Furniture against a
wall can feel cold some-
times, like a high school
dance where everybody is
standing around the perimeter of the gym."

—Vicente Wolf

DRESS UP YOUR ENTRY

Go for big gestures. Paint it a rich dark color, and put in comfortable seating and a big mirror. Guests might never make it to the living room!

DRESS UP YOUR PATIO
A big skirted ottoman adds a touch of indoor elegance to the outdoors.

REPURPOSE IT

An antique bookcase makes a splendid bar, don't you think? And those mirrored cabinet doors, the mirrored edges: Steal the look!

◄ A Louis-Philippe commode was fitted with a small sink to create a masculine vanity. The antique French chair was reupholstered in cotton-cashmere, giving it a modern twist.

The velvet upholstery on Podge Bune's sofa "used to be curtains I did for a client who got married to a very modern wife."

BUY NEW SHEETS

"My favorites are white hotel-style sheets with a colored border—they have such a classic look. You can buy them anywhere," says Eric Cohler.

DESIGNER *tip!*

"New bedding can make a bedroom feel fresh and new again. Areahome.com or dwellstudio.com have gorgeous and sophisticated sheets that won't empty your wallet."

—Eve Robinson

RESTACK YOUR PILLOWS

Stacking your pillows in different ways. Here, smaller pillows line up vertically in descending height, while Euro pillows lie horizontally.

CARVE OUT A WORK SPACE

A mudroom doubles as a home office, with an Arts and Crafts-inspired desk and a vintage metal chair.

DESIGNER *tip!*

"Turn a closet into a home office. Take off the door. Make a huge bulletin board for the wall. If you can, nudge in the perfect Parsons desk from westelm.com."

—Amanda Nisbet

IN A SUNNY SPOT

A simple folding table in front of a window is all it takes to make an inviting workspace.

IN THE LIVING ROOM

An ebony-and-gilt painted writing table and a fringed yellow stool makes a sexy and sophisticated work space behind a sofa.

◄ MAKE IT INSPIRING
Rev up your creative juices with inspiration boards.

THE BIGGER, THE BETTER
A larger room achieves balance with scale, like the Noguchi lantern—four feet in diameter—the lamps, the sculpture on the coffee table.

DOCTOR IT UP

Kelly Van Patter wanted to be as thrifty as possible, so she got her island from Ikea. "I covered the butcher block top in stainless steel, painted the frame gray, and replaced the grating in the bottom with a piece of wood. Then I put casters on it."

INSTANT BEDSIDE TABLE
Vintage suitcases on wood blocks are topped with a tray.

DESIGNER
tip!

"In smaller kitchens, I add heavy-duty casters to the table, so you can move it out of the way. I really like the industrial look, and the rubber won't scratch floors. The brake is essential to hold the table in place."

—Steven Scalaroff

"Put a striped rug over your solid—color rug to create a new feeling in any room."

—SCOTT SANDERS.

"A CLIENT HAD OLD, FADED SOFAS, BUT THEY HAD GOOD LINES— SO I JUST SLIPCOVERED THEM IN CRISP WHITE LINEN AND THEY BECAME NEW AND MODERN."

—ALEXANDRA CHAMPALIMAUD

"I like to make simple slipcovers for my square headboard—white linen for summer, velvet for winter. It's so easy: cut out a front and a back, and stitch them together."

—EMILY HENRY

"I draped a Mongolian lamb's wool throw over my lumpy old sofa and suddenly it was luxurious and exotic."

—DAVID MANN

"TRY EDISON BULBS IN YOUR SCONCES AND CHANDELIERS. DITCH THE SHADES FOR A MORE MODERN LOOK."

—PHILIP GORRIVAN

"Swap out the mats on your framed photos to a brighter color. Or do a double mat with another color peeking through. You'll see your pictures in a new way."

—JEAN LARRETTE

"Add a glass top to a table for a more sophisticated look. You can put fabric or wallpaper underneath, or even paint the underside of the glass to give it a little more jazz."

—KENDALL WILKINSON

"TO MODERNIZE A TRADITIONAL, OLD-WORLD ROOM, ALL YOU NEED IS A NEW STAINLESS-STEEL TABLE, A GLASS LAMP, OR A CONTEMPORARY CHAIR. YOU DON'T HAVE TO CHANGE THE WHOLE ROOM."

—GINGER BARBER

SIMPLIFY*it!*

LESSON FROM THE MASTER

The dean of decorating—the late Albert Hadley—helped a client with her fresh start: downsizing to a smaller house. They were a perfect match: His look was clean, and she can't stand clutter. "I never keep anything I don't want," she says. Her living room speaks for itself. (Take note: Painting a floor white is one of the easiest ways to freshen a room.)

CLEAN AND SPARE

There's not a hint of fussiness in this country-house living room by Jesse Carrier and Mara Miller. "We don't add extraneous details. We tend to edit out rather than put in," says Miller. "I think there's a level of comfort in that plainness," Carrier adds. "What you see is what you get."

"Simplify, de-clutter, and see your rooms anew. If you have something you don't like, get rid of it today!"

—Matthew White

NO FRILLS, NO FROUFROU

If a monastery had a luxury suite, it would probably look something like this
bedroom. One painting, one pillowless white chair, one small rug, a starkly geometric
tester bed with no canopy or bed curtains, and the quiet glow of golden-yellow walls.

A GAUZY WHITE HIDEAWAY

Architect Bill Ingram skipped the curtains on his bedroom windows and put them on his tester bed instead. "I used Belgian linen sheers. They're not exactly mosquito netting, but they make you think of that."

FROM SO-SO TO SO SLEEK

"Pristine white, clean lines, symmetry, neatness: that's what I call serenity," says Lindsey Bond. She removed the moldings and the mantel in her living room for a cleaner, crisper, fresher look. "Unless they're fabulous, mantels and moldings are just clutter." Two floating shelves add to the airy lightness. "To me, a running horizontal line of shelves looks like the horizon—so peaceful." To add interest she painted a band of slightly darker white that starts at the baseboard and goes up 30 inches: a super-simplified version of wainscoting.

◀ In Bond's bedroom, the floating desk and Louis Ghost chair keep bulky and leggy furniture to a minimum. Curtains framing the antiqued mirror hide her closet door, a TV, and electrical cords.

Bond's simple floating shelf in the back entry not only gives her a convenient dropoff for keys and sunglasses, it's another opportunity to show off art and hold vases filled with branches or flowers to cheer up the space.

ENJOY THE SHINE

A rugless, highly polished floor—and a huge antique mirrored panel—bring luminosity to a living room.

DESIGNER *tip!*

"Rip up the old wall-to-wall and bare the wood floors. Clean and wax them to a shine. Sit back and enjoy the new spacious feeling."

—Lee Bierly

◄ RECYCLE THE RUG

In her living room, Jill Sharp Brinson put the hide on the sofa instead of on the floor—which she left bare. (Note the way the folded throw adds a feminine band of pink.)

Brinson also draped her dining table with white hide, softening its industrial edge. The room has a soothing, dreamy aura. "I love the cabinets," she says. "I did three layers of white mixed with gray, and a spray-on lacquer finish. And I love seeing dishes through the chicken wire."

INSTANT HEADBOARD

Erin Martin's simple and stunning solution for the guest room headboard: "A suzani, just a pretty one behind the bed, and you're done!" She tied it casually to hooks for a relaxed look.

CASUAL ELEGANCE

Wicker furniture, sisal, and simple window treatments have a young, unpretentious air about them. "I always gravitate to oil-rubbed bronze rods and rings. They help define the window and add balance to other dark things in a space," says Lindsay Reid.

◄ RUG HUMILITY
Chinese rush matting covers the floor of a room in an 18th-century house. Even Thomas Jefferson used it at Monticello.

SIMPLE AND SEE-THROUGH ➤
A bamboo curtain hung across a doorway lends a breezy island feeling to a home office.

RUG POWER
You don't have to fill a big room with furniture. One big graphic rug will tame it.

"*Rent a Dumpster and prune, prune, prune! If you take a day and actually look at the things in your house, you'll realize that a million of them can be tossed.*"

—JONATHAN ADLER

"PURGE, EDIT, AND ORGANIZE YOUR CLOSET. WE LOVE BEAUTIFUL LINEN-COVERED BOXES IN DIFFERENT SIZES, SHAPES, AND COLORS TO RESPOND TO THE DIFFERENT CATEGORIES OF YOUR POSSESSIONS. BUY ALL NEW HANGERS. ADD A PERSONAL ACCENT, LIKE SCENTED SHELF LINERS."

—ELISSA CULLMAN

"I like to do this myself at least once a year. Take every last loose piece on every surface—photos, vases, candlesticks, magazines—whatever is cluttering up your vision and that chances are you no longer see. Put them on a counter in the kitchen, then redeploy in new arrangements. But only use half of them. Put the rest into a closet for a free shopping spree the next time around."

—JAMIE DRAKE

"LOVING STUFF IS NOT THE SAME AS DISPLAYING STUFF. ACCESSORIES ARE LIKE A WOMAN'S JEWELRY. YOU WOULD NEVER WEAR ALL OF IT AT ONCE. OUR RULE OF THUMB IS TO EDIT YOUR ACCESSORIES SO THAT YOU NEVER HAVE MORE THAN 20 PERCENT OUT AT A GIVEN TIME."

—DAN BARSANTI

"I ONCE HAD A FRIEND
STAY WITH ME FOR A WEEK
AND SHE CLEANED OUT ALL
MY DRAWERS. IT WAS A
LIFE-CHANGING EXPERIENCE.
SO GO TO THE CONTAINER
STORE AND BUY ALL THOSE
DRAWER DIVIDERS AND
START ORGANIZING."

—PHOEBE HOWARD

"Clean your
bathroom counters of
everything except your
prettiest essentials."

—JEAN LARRETTE

"Put your favorite
family photos in frames
of just one material—sterling,
silver plate—to avoid clutter.
For pictures of less good
looking relatives, God
invented albums."

—JOE NYE

"When we got a puppy, we
casually draped and tucked
those white canvas painter's
drop cloths over the furniture.
It calmed everything
down and looked so good that
we kept them on a lot
longer than we had to."

—JASON BELL

PHOTOGRAPHY CREDITS

William Abranowicz: 24, 123, 132 bottom

Christopher Baker: 40 top, 80

Roger Davies: 228-229

Reed Davis: 100 bottom, 101, 136, 142, 178-179, 198, 201, 275

Pieter Estersohn: 203

Tria Giovan: 10, 46, 150

John Hall: 235

Ken Hayden: 200

Alec Hemer: 117

Matthew Hranek: 53

Ditte Isager/ Edge Reps: 28 bottom, 108, 148, 234

Thibault Jeanson: 3, 128-129, 130-131, 186-187

John Kernick: 52, 209

Francesco Lagnese: vi-vii, xii, 2, 31, 34-35, 36, 44, 56, 72, 78, 85, 98, 99, 104, 121, 122, 126, 143, 144, 152, 168, 193, 208, 212, 214-215, 222, 224, 226-227, 232, 243, 277

David Duncan Livingston: 114-115

Thomas Loof: ii, 4, 9, 22-23, 25 bottom right, 29, 30, 38-39, 45, 47, 66, 81, 90-91, 110, 139, 145, 149, 151, 167, 176, 181, 213, 220-221, 254 top, 269

Ellen McDermott: 18-19, 21, 40 bottom, 244

Maura McEvoy: 86, 166

Josh McHugh: 6-7

James Merrell: 25 top left, 41, 48, 59, 89, 127, 210-211

Ngoc Minh Ngo: 60, 61, 65, 79, 97, 156, 165, 182-183, 225

INDEX